The D

Wood

By

Ken Mackenzie

Special thanks to Joy Harris for helping with the editing and to Sue Hawkins for the illustrations

First Published 2017 HawkMedia Publishing

53 Stucley Road
Bideford
Devon
Ex393eq

© Ken Mackenzie 2017

ISBN-13: 978-1545125380
ISBN-10: 1545125384

The Dark Wood

Website: www.hawkmedia.co.uk

Email:admin@hawkmedia.co.uk

Telephone: 01237 476238

About The Author

" KENNY MAC,"
Torquay children's author.

Every day in Pixie Wood was a summer's day. The sun always shone and there was never a dark cloud in the sky. The pixies and fairies that lived in the wood were always happy and spent all day playing and having lots of fun. It was a very, very happy place.

Bapoo was the king of the pixies and lived in a grand castle at the top of the highest tree in Pixie Wood where he could see everything and everyone.

One bright and sunny day, as Bapoo was watching all the pixies and fairies playing games, he noticed smoke coming from the place they called the Dark Wood. This was a faraway place that none of those who lived in Pixie Wood had ever seen. It was a place where the sun never shone so it was always dark and cold.

King Bapoo called for his strongest pixie guard to come to the castle to see him.
"I have seen smoke coming from the Dark Wood," said the king. "I want you to travel as fast as you can and see why there is smoke."

His strongest pixie packed himself a lunch of bread and berries and set off on his journey.

2

Two full days passed before the strongest pixie returned. He was very dirty and hungry and tired. "My king," he said, "there are giants in the dark wood who are chopping down all the trees and setting fire to them."

"Giants?" asked the king. "What kind of giants?"

"They are called people, my king, and there are many of them. They have giant machines and they are coming this way."

The king was very worried as he had never seen giants before and he couldn't understand why they were chopping down and burning trees. He then decided he would have to go and see for himself. Maybe he could talk to the giants for after all, he was a king.

He called all the pixies and all the fairies together in his castle and told them what the giants were doing. This made everyone very, very afraid but the king told them not to worry because he was going to speak to them himself.

The next day, his strongest pixie saddled two mice from the stables and packed bread and berries and water in the saddle bags. The king climbed onto the white mouse and his strongest pixie climbed onto the black one.

3

They waved goodbye to all the pixies and fairies who had come to wish them well on their journey and they headed towards the Dark Wood.

They scampered through the wood for a long time and passed lots of woodland creatures like rabbits, birds and squirrels along the way.

By the middle of the day, the wood was very quiet and there were no more animals to be seen. This puzzled the king who turned to his strongest pixie and said, "I don't understand why we haven't seen any animals for some time. Perhaps we should stop and have some lunch and think about this."

They pulled their mice to a stop, climbed down and tied their reins to some strong stalks of grass. Then they unpacked the bread and berries and water and started to eat their lunch.

"Strongest Pixie," said the king, "where do you think all the animals have gone?"

"Your majesty, perhaps the giants are close and have frightened all the woodland creatures away?" said the strongest pixie.

Suddenly, they heard a rustling sound coming from the bushes close by and they turned to see a red-brown face with a pointy nose, pointy ears and big brown eyes. It was a young fox.

5

"Your majesty," said the fox, "I've been following you for a while to make sure you find the giants. The other creatures stay away because they are too afraid but the fox families have been watching them from their secret places. If you follow me, I'll take you there."

"Thank you fox," said the king. "We'll be pleased to follow you."

The strongest pixie packed the rest of the food and drink away into the saddle bags and loosened the reins. Then he and the king climbed onto their mice and followed the fox through the dark, quiet wood.

At the end of the day, the fox stopped and pointed to an empty space through the trees. "That's where the giants are," he said, "and now I must be on my way. I will tell the other creatures that you have found them. Goodbye and thank you for helping us all."

The king and the strongest pixie steered their mice slowly through the space between the trees and saw that the giants were indeed chopping down and burning all the trees.

The king then climbed down from his white mouse and stood on the biggest mushroom he could find.

At the top of his voice he shouted, "Stop, I command you to stop!" The giants, however, could not hear him because he was so small. Again he shouted, "Stop, I command you to stop!" but still the machines kept knocking down the trees and still the giants were setting fire to them.

"What shall we do?" asked his strongest pixie.

"We will return to Pixie Wood and I will speak to Matoo, the wise owl, for he will know what to do."
When the king got back to his castle he sent for Matoo to come and see him.

Matoo was a very, very old owl who had lived in Pixie Wood for a very, very, very long time and who was very, very wise.

The king told Matoo what he had seen. Matoo was very quiet for a moment as he thought about what the king had told him. Then he said,

"I know of these giants, and I know what they can do. They will destroy all of the trees, then they will build houses for other giants to live in. If we are to save our homes, we must speak with them.

We must tell them about our wood, for if they are able to destroy a place of beauty, then they must be able to understand the consequences of what they do."

9

"You are indeed very wise," said the king, and he declared that everyone in Pixie Wood must come to his castle straight away.

The whole of Pixie Wood gathered at the castle that very day and the king told them what Matoo had said. They were all very afraid, all except one.

"I will go to the Dark Wood and speak with them," said a little voice from the back of the room.

"Who said that?" asked the king.

"It was me sire, Forrick."

"And who is Forrick?" asked the king.

"I am your berry picker. I collect the berries for your dinner every day."

The king smiled, "And just how will you stop these giants and their machines?"

"I do not know my king but I will try."

The king was very quiet for a few moments and then he said, "Who will go with Forrick to speak with the giants?"

Not one raised their hand. Nobody wanted to go to the Dark Wood.

"Then I will go alone," said Forrick.

Suddenly, a voice they all knew said, "I will stand with you Forrick, for you are the bravest pixie in this land." It was none other than Matoo, the wise old owl. He said, "I have seen too many years to know that battles are not always won by strength alone. To win this battle will need courage and this is a lesson you must learn Forrick. Climb onto my back and I will take you to the Dark Wood."

The king made sure that Matoo and Forrick were given plenty of food and water and the whole of Pixie Wood watched them leave for the Dark Wood, just as the sun was setting.

Matoo and Forrick travelled all through the night and they arrived at the Dark Wood just before the sun rose. It was still very dark and it was very quiet as all the giants were asleep.

Forrick looked around in shock at all the burned trees and the sleeping giant machines and where were the animals? "In Pixie Wood, there are lots of different animals like rabbits and birds and foxes," he said to Matoo, "but here there are none."

"I fear they have all gone deep into the forest," said Matoo. "And now it is time for me to leave you," he said. "I wish you luck on this great adventure and remember Forrick, you can achieve anything if you have the courage." With a great flap of his wings, Matoo rose into the sky and was gone.

Forrick was now alone and he sat down on a small stone to think. He wondered how just speaking to the giants would make them stop. Would they listen to him or would they carry on until they had burnt down Pixie Wood? He didn't know the answer but he did know that he had to keep his promise to the king. This made him determined to speak to the giants in the morning and that was his last thought before his eyes got heavy and he fell asleep, for it had been a long, long night.

The sun began to climb over the trees, and it wasn't long before the giants started to arrive. Forrick was awakened to a crashing sound as the huge machines began knocking down the trees and the giants started sawing them into little pieces. He was very afraid when he saw fire and smoke and when he heard lots and lots of noise as the trees crashed to the ground and the giant machines rumbled through the dark woods. Yes, he was very afraid, but he had to keep his promise to try and stop the giants from reaching Pixie Wood.

Forrick picked up his knapsack with the berries and bread given to him by the king and headed towards the sound of the crashing and banging.

He hadn't gone very far when there in front of him was a large wooden building with huge windows and the biggest door he had ever seen. He decided that this must be where the king of the giants lived, for he had never seen a wooden castle as big as this.

Forrick pushed with all of his might on the giant wooden door, but he was so tiny that the door did not budge one bit. He tried banging on the door as hard as he could but no matter how hard he banged, no-one could hear it above the noise of the machines and cutting things.

Poor Forrick didn't know what to do, how could he speak with the king of the giants if he couldn't even get into their castle? He sat down on the giant step and could only watch as the big machines continued cutting and chopping.

Suddenly, Forrick heard a noise behind him. He turned around and looked up to see that there, standing over him, was a giant. Forrick was so afraid that he just sat and stared at the giant whose head seemed to reach into the clouds.

"What's this?" said the giant and bent down to get a closer look at Forrick. "What is this strange little creature?" it said. The giant slowly reached down and picked Forrick up. Poor Forrick could do nothing to save himself, he just closed his eyes, held his breath and awaited his fate, for he feared he would surely be crushed just like the flowers in the woods had been.

Slowly, the giant's hand opened. Forrick opened one eye, "Oh my goodness," he thought, "I will surely be gobbled up for dinner." He slowly opened his other eye and looked up to see the face of the giant. It was smiling. Forrick wasn't sure if he should be happy or frightened but at least he hadn't been eaten up.

"Hello," said the giant. It was a little girl with bright red hair.

"Hello," said Forrick quietly.

"And what are you?" asked the girl.

"I am a pixie," he said quietly. "My name is Forrick. Please don't eat me."

The little girl giggled, "I won't eat you," she said. "My name is Anna. I have never seen a pixie before. Do you live here?"

"No," said Forrick, and he told her his story.

The little girl listened, then she said, "We have no king here and that castle is just an old garden shed. We are not giants, we are just bigger than you. You have nothing to fear from us."

"But the giants are chopping and cutting all the trees," said Forrick.

"They are not giants," she said. "They are my mummy and daddy and my aunt. They are just clearing the old wood and the dead trees so the sun can shine through."

Forrick was no longer afraid of the giants and Anna seemed to be very kind. She gently put Forrick in her lunch box and went to where her family was still cutting down the weeds and dead wood. She told them of Forrick's brave journey and his quest to save Pixie Wood.

Her mummy and daddy and aunt immediately stopped work. They were amazed to see a real live pixie. They had read about them when they were children but always thought they were just in stories. They were so happy to know they had a whole village of pixies in the woods.

Anna's daddy took the lunch box with Forrick still inside and put it in his car. "I will take Forrick to the far side of the woods," he said. "He can tell his king that there will be no more cutting and chopping and that their village is quite safe," and off they went.

It was just coming up to lunch time when Anna's daddy arrived at the place Forrick had told him about. He took the lunch box and placed it on the ground. Forrick climbed out and thanked the giant.

"My king and my people will be so pleased when I tell them the news I have," said Forrick."

"Tell them they have nothing to fear from us," said Anna's daddy.

Forrick ran as fast as he could and soon arrived at the king's castle. He told the king about Anna and her family and how they had stopped clearing the woods.

The king was very pleased and the whole of Pixie Wood celebrated the bravery of Forrick.

Thanks to Anna and her family, all the dead wood and weeds have now gone, the sun shines through the tree tops and the whole of the wood is bathed in bright sunshine.

The king made Forrick his head berry picker and he is no longer just a little voice at the back of the room. He showed that you can do anything if you only have the courage to try.

The End

Thankyou!!
I hope you enjoyed this story.

Printed in Great Britain
by Amazon